IMAGES
of America

GARDEN
GROVE

The Tower on the Green, dedicated on April 18, 2002, is located at the corner of Main and Euclid Streets. Sponsored by the Garden Grove Community Association and made possible through donations by individuals, organizations, businesses, and the City, the tower and clock have become familiar landmarks.

IMAGES
of America

GARDEN
GROVE

Garden Grove Historical Society

ARCADIA
PUBLISHING

Published by Arcadia Publishing
Charleston, South Carolina

Library of Congress Catalog Card Number: 2005924670

For all general information contact Arcadia Publishing at:
Telephone 843-853-2070
Fax 843-853-0044
E-mail sales@arcadiapublishing.com
For customer service and orders:
Toll-Free 1-888-313-2665

Visit us on the Internet at www.arcadiapublishing.com

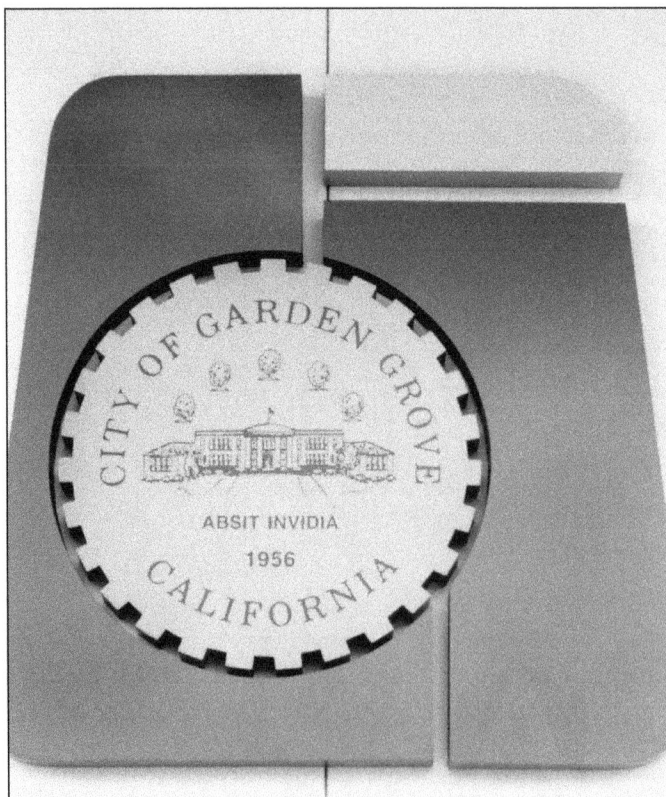

The seal of the City of Garden Grove appears at the entrance to city hall. The Latin phrase translates to "Without Malice," but the City uses a paraphrased translation: "May There Be No Envy or Ill Will."

CONTENTS

ACKNOWLEDGMENTS

This book has been made possible with the help of many people. What started out as a project to find and track down enough suitable pictures ended up being a decision-making project on what to keep and what had to be left out. Assembling the pictures brought back memories to many of the old-timers who were here when the area had a more rural atmosphere and who experienced the rapid growth as Garden Grove became a mature city. Listing all the people who helped with this publication would be impossible. Without them taking pictures over the 131 years of Garden Grove's existence, no book could be done; however, special thanks must be given to the members of the Garden Grove Historical Society who spent many hours in the preparation of the material. These include Jo Ann and Terry Thomas, Beulah Miller, Virginia Carter, Carol Schnitger, Udo and Eva Ahrndt, and Steve Smith. Most of the pictures appearing in this book are from the historical society's collection, but those that were loaned for inclusion in the book are credited beneath each image. Thanks to you all. Please enjoy a bit of the history of our diverse community of Garden Grove.

INTRODUCTION

Spanish soldiers commanded by Gaspar de Portola first discovered the area known today as Orange County as they made their way north across California in 1769. During their journey, the soldiers camped on a wide, grassy plain east of present-day Garden Grove. They named the area Santa Ana Valley and claimed California as a possession of Spain. Manuel Nieto first owned the area by virtue of a Spanish land grant. It was later subdivided into large ranchos, many of which were bought by the great land baron Abel Stearns.

The settlement of Garden Grove was mostly within the Rancho Las Bolsas, which included 33,000 acres, claimed the Santa Ana River as its eastern boundary, and stretched to the Pacific Ocean on the south. Following several years of floods and droughts, the rancho era came to an end and the homespun spirit of westward expansion took over. With the breakup of the large ranchos, families came and settled in the general area of what is now Garden Grove.

In 1874, Dr. Alonzo Cook arrived in the area and purchased 160 acres of land for about $15 an acre. Recognized as Garden Grove's founding father, he donated land northwest of what is now Main Street and Garden Grove Boulevard for use as a site for a schoolhouse and post office. A simple one-room school was constructed and was in use for about 10 years. According to local tradition, Dr. Cook suggested the name "Garden Grove" for the school and surrounding village. Some people countered that the name did not fit the open terrain. Cook responded, "We'll make it appropriate by planting trees and making it beautiful."

The village of Garden Grove was originally part of Los Angeles County. It normally required two-days travel time for a round trip to the county seat in Los Angeles. However, as more people moved into the area, the great distance they had to travel to county offices to conduct business caused the residents to start action for the formation of a new county. In 1889, an election was held and the new County of Orange was voted into existence. When the County of Orange was formed, the Garden Grove area had a population of about 200. It continued as a quiet farming community into the 20th century, but in 1905 the village era came to an end and the town era of Garden Grove began.

In 1905, the Pacific Electric Railway with their red cars came to Garden Grove, bringing visitors and settlers and a way for local farmers to ship their harvest to distant markets. Packing houses were established along the railroad to help farmers process and ship the bounty from their farms, and Garden Grove became a shipping center for the surrounding area. Agriculture continued as the town's main economy for the next 40 years, until World War II. Oranges, walnuts, chili peppers, sugar beets, and lima beans were some of the more important crops of local farms. Adding to the mix of agricultural products, poultry ranches and egg production became very popular, lasting until the postwar housing boom.

Servicemen who had visited California during their training for the war came back to settle and rear their families, creating a great demand for housing in much of Southern California. This demand, available land, relatively low prices, and reasonably close proximity to major industry caused a building boom in the early 1950s in the Garden Grove area. In fact, Garden Grove was the fastest-growing city in the nation for several years in the 1950s and early 1960s. This sudden growth brought the need for a more formal government structure. Finally, after several attempts to incorporate the community over a period of many years, an election was held on April 17, 1956, and was successful. On June 15, 1956, the Orange County Board of Supervisors passed a resolution declaring that the City of Garden Grove was a legal entity and the secretary of state made it official on June 18, 1956.

Today, the community is a dynamic and thriving city with a strong sense of its roots and its colorful history. The city has a good mix of business and industry as well as strong residential neighborhoods. From the beginning and continuing today, there has also been a strong religious influence. Churches of several faiths started almost as soon as the community began to form; today's Crystal Cathedral is world renowned. The school district is one of the largest in the state and has received numerous awards for excellence. There are branches of several colleges located in the city as well. Garden Grove has become an ethnically diverse city with growing populations from many backgrounds. Hispanic and Japanese citizens were early settlers in the Garden Grove area and established farms by the 1920s. Korean and Vietnamese citizens have established districts and are bringing their culture to be part of Garden Grove. Come take a visit by browsing through the pictures of our village growing into a town and becoming a modern city.

NOTE: Several street names within the city have changed over the years. Street names used in the captions generally refer to the name that was in use at the time of the picture. When Euclid Street was realigned to connect to Verano Street at Garden Grove Boulevard in 1965, the last few blocks of the original Euclid Street was named Main Street and Verano became Euclid Street. Ocean Avenue became Garden Grove Boulevard during the town period.

One

THE EARLY DEVELOPMENT YEARS

1874–1920

Alonzo Gary Cook is considered to have founded Garden Grove in 1874, although there were scattered families in the area before that time. Cook built a home on a 10-acre parcel of his original 160-acre purchase at the southeast corner of Nelson Street and Lampson Avenue, and lived there for about six years. He sold the property in 1880 and seems to have left the area in 1881, as no further record of him is found. During his short stay, Cook was instrumental in providing a school in 1874; a church in 1875; and the general store, the post office, and a blacksmith shop around 1877.

Eucalyptus groves such as this one were planted in hopes of providing lumber. The wood proved unsatisfactory for this purpose, but the trees found great use as windbreaks for orchards and farms. Another use for the trees was found in the leaves, which were boiled to make eucalyptus oil, and this became one of the first industries in Garden Grove. A few rows of eucalyptus trees still define old property lines and boundaries of early orchards. The workers in this *c.* 1900 photo are cutting trees (for firewood) and stripping the leaves.

Vats like this, with a copper liner, were used to boil eucalyptus leaves to extract their oil for medicine. Photographed around 1960, this vat may be found today on the grounds of Mitchell School, located on Taft Street at Trask Avenue.

On the right is a La Marque (white) rose at the home of early resident E.G. Ware. Planted in 1883, it measured 22 inches in circumference near the root in 1889. By June 1894, it measured 26 inches. Pictured c. 1900 are Mary Ware, on the left, and her daughter L. Agnes Ware.

METHODIST CHURCH.

GARD
LOS A

This sketch was included in an 1886 publicity booklet titled "Orange Illustrated and Its Surroundings." The booklet helped promote the "Boom of the 1880s." The spots on the left

PUBLIC SCHOOL

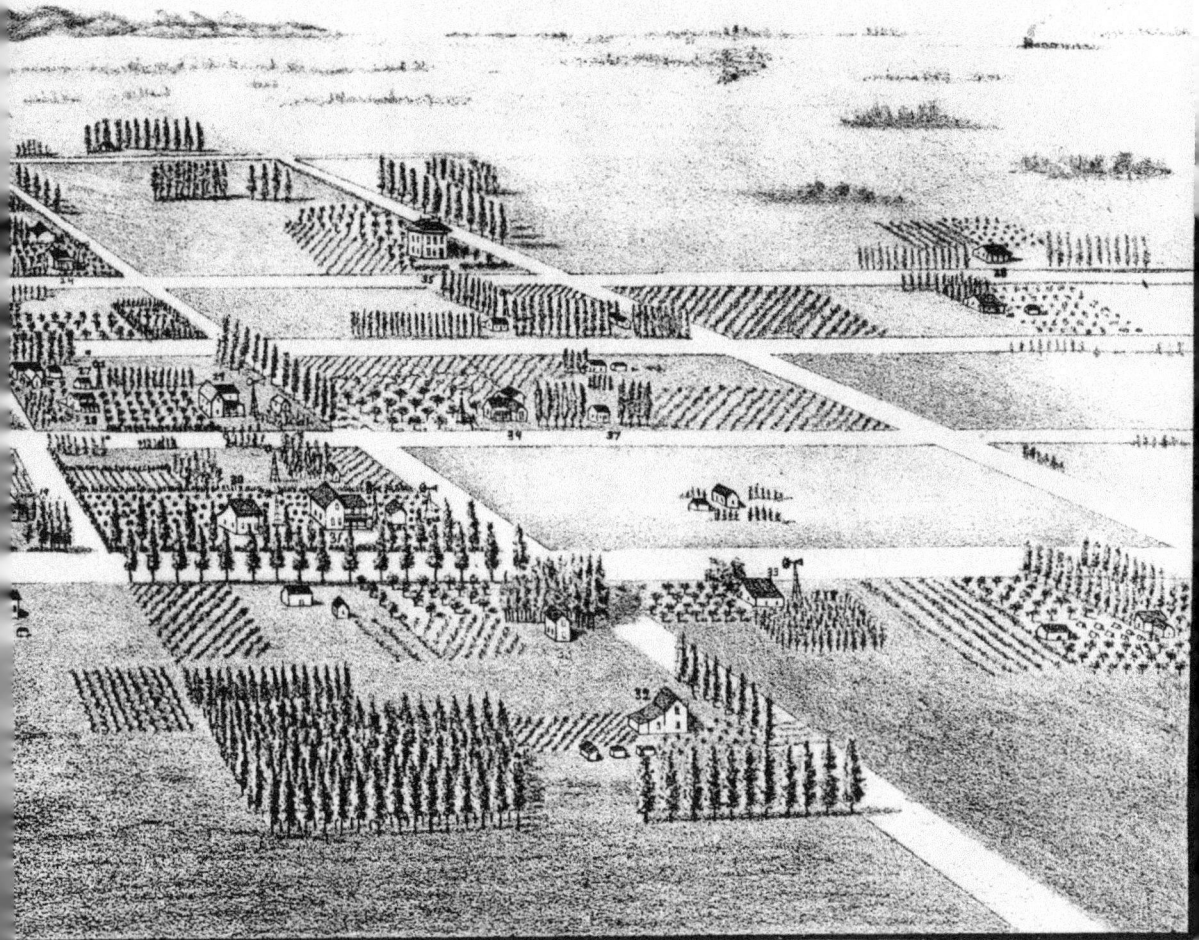

20 MRS DAVIS	25 D B CHAFFEE	30 O G HOUGH	35 L J FELTON
21 A T CHAFFEE	26 W S BRADLEY	31 J WARNER	36 G O WARE
22 D HITCHCOCK	27 J HILL	32 SMITH	37 HAWKINS
23 W R FARRINGTON	28 J D CHAFFEE	33 REV J M RICH	38 WHITE
24 F J RODGERS	29 C P BESSONETT	34 B STURGIS	A PACIFIC OCEAN

horizon are ships off the coast.

13

Pictured *c.* 1885 is the home of early settlers Charles and Lois Hitchcock. In an attempt to gain ownership of their property, the penniless Fred Anschlag murdered them on January 23, 1888. Anschlag was arrested and held in an Anaheim corncrib overnight to evade the lynch mob that had stormed the jail. Anschlag had decided to purchase the Hitchcock place and made a $25 deposit even though he had little in the way of funds. Apparently, his desire for the property outweighed his lack of financial resources. The irony was that Mr. Hitchcock had executed the deed and had it in his possession, ready for delivery, when the murder took place.

Shown here is the envelope and invitation to the hanging of Fred Anschlag. After his murder conviction, Anschlag was jailed in Los Angeles, where he escaped his hanging by taking poison two days before the scheduled event.

OFFICE OF THE SHERIFF LOS ANGELES CO., CAL.
Los Angeles City, November 8, 1888.

Mr. *A J Chaffee*

Dear Sir: You are respectfully invited to be present at the execution of

John Henrich Frederick Anschlag,

which will take place at the County Jail of this County on Friday, the 16th of November, A.D., 1888, at one o'clock, p. m.

PRESENT THIS AT THE SIDE DOOR OF THE JAIL YARD. VISITORS ARE REQUESTED TO ABSTAIN FROM SMOKING, LOUD TALKING, AND ALL IMPROPER CONDUCT.

JAMES C. KAYS,

NOT TRANSFERABLE.   Sheriff.

The home of early resident Edward Chaffee, pictured here c. 1900, stood on the east side of Nelson Street, south of Stanford Avenue. The home was torn down in the 1980s to make way for new housing.

This group of local residents pictured on a c. 1900 camping trip includes, from left to right, (seated) Alonzo Chaffee, Dorr B. Chaffee, John D. Chaffee, and Albert Chaffee; (standing) Mr. ? Lane, Mr. ? Sanford, Reverend Burton, Mr. ? Zavitz, and Ernest Chaffee. The Chaffee brothers were very early residents of Garden Grove.

16

Bolsa Grande School, pictured here in 1891, was one of several elementary schools in the Garden Grove area. It was formed in 1870, although no settlement was near it for another 20 years. In 1874, the Garden Grove Elementary School District was created out of part of the Bolsa Grande District.

Alamitos Elementary School is shown here with its students in 1891. The Alamitos School District, organized in 1878, was located a little over three miles west of the Garden Grove School. Alamitos Elementary School was located at the corner of Magnolia Street and Chapman Avenue. The Alamitos and Garden Grove Districts merged on July 1, 1965.

17

Local citizens gather *c.* 1912 at the intersection of Euclid Street and Ocean Avenue to welcome the Anaheim Merchants Association. (Courtesy of Don Dobmeier.)

This *c.* 1907 street scene, looking north, shows the Garden Grove Hotel on the right. The cross street is Ocean Avenue. By 1912, these dirt streets were paved.

In the 1880s, this Harper Johnson subdivision map became the first document of its kind to be recorded in the history of Garden Grove. It was not a successful development and the map had to be revised in 1891.

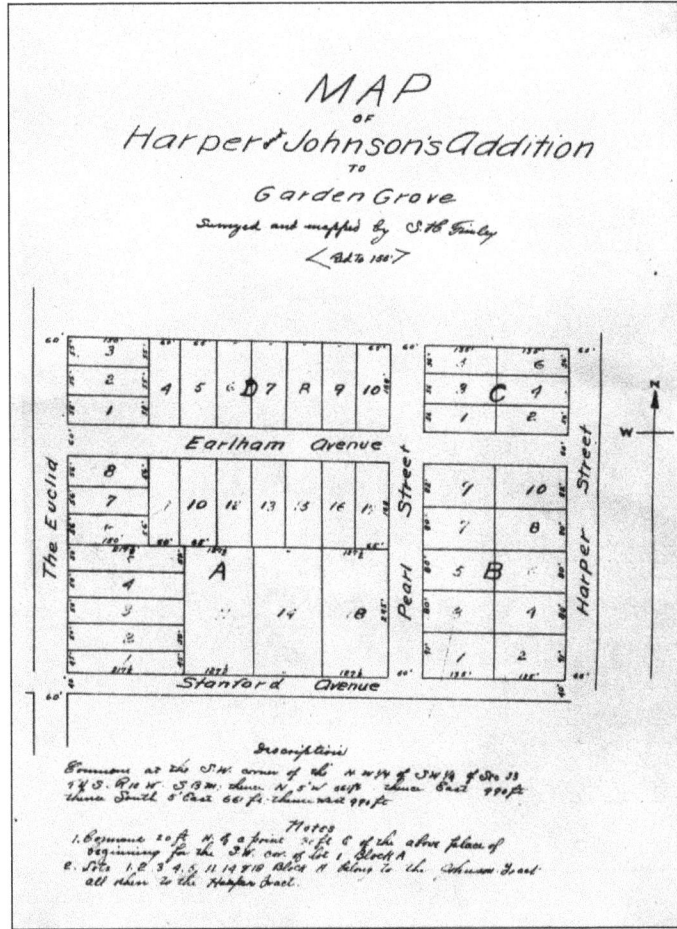

This was the Garden Grove entry in the 1885 Flower Show held in Santa Ana.

The second Garden Grove school building was located on the west side of Euclid Street, just north of the original one-room school. This two-room school, which housed a large meeting hall on the second floor, opened for the 1884–1885 school year. Its yard extended nearly to Acacia Avenue. The school was in use until 1908, when the Lincoln School opened. This building was then torn down, and the lumber was salvaged and reused for other local construction projects. The bell now resides at the Stanley Ranch Museum.

Garden Grove School students posed for this 1891 picture. Note that most of the boys are barefoot. The school provided instruction through the ninth grade.

The 1891 ninth-grade graduation class of the Garden Grove School was the school's first. Pictured, from left to right, are Mettie Chaffee, Mary Lawton, Bertha Robinson, William Mitchell, Estelle Woodman, and Walter Hill.

MOTTO—"Thus Ends Our First Lesson."

Programme.

You are invited to be present at the

Commencement Exercises

of the

Garden Grove School

to be held at

Schoolhouse Hall,

Tuesday eve'ng, June 16, '91,

at 8 o'clock.

Orange Post Print,

Organ Voluntary...Miss Ella Dishe

Prayer..Rev. Sprowl

Salutatory and Essay–"Object of Life".........Mettie E. Chaffe

Quartette.."We Come With Song
    Miss Mina Robinson, Mrs. Geo. Chaffee,
    Messrs. R. J. Young, and R. B. Robinson.

Oration–"Progress in Improvements".............Wm. M. Mitchel

Essay–"Pussy Wants a Corner".....................Mary E. Lawto

Vocal Solo–"The Song That Reached My Heart"..Mrs. Geo. Chaffe

Oration–"Little Things".................................Walter B. Hil

Essay–"Our English Ancestors"..............A. Bertha Robinso

Octette.."Merrily Goes Our Bark
    Misses Fannie Chaffee, Estelle Woodman, Emma King, Mary
    Lawton, Messrs. Hill, Rich, Hilliker, Yoder.

Essay–"Self-made Men"..............................Mabel A. Townsen

Essay–"Night Brings Out the Stars"............H. Estelle Woodma

Vocal Solo–"Sweet Mignonette".................Miss Nina Robinso

Valedictory...Walter B. Hil

Presentation of Diplomas..........................Dr. H. W. Hea

Address...J. P. Yode

Music.."Farewe
    Misses Mary Lawton, Emma King, Estelle Woodman, Fannie
    Chaffee, Messrs. Wm. Hilliker, Walter Hill.

The invitation and program for the 1891 graduating class provides a list of many of the early Garden Grove families. The graduation took place on the second floor of the school.

Walter B. Harper, the village blacksmith, is shown with some of the tools of his trade. His shop was located on the corner of Acacia Avenue and Euclid Street. George Little, the area's first blacksmith, founded his shop at this same location in 1877.

Walter Harper (in the white shirt) and his cousin Henry Seaman are shown inside the Harper Blacksmith Shop, c. 1916.

In this *c.* 1910 photograph, workers are surrounded by flats for drying apricots on the Leonard Ranch. The track and car made moving the flats much easier.

Sugar beets became a major farm crop in the late 1880s. Shown here around 1895 is an early beet processing plant.

The Butler and Kenah Livery, pictured here around 1900, was one of several stables in the area.

David Webster, Garden Grove's first postmaster, is pictured c. 1891 in front of the first post office building at the corner of Euclid Street and Stanford Avenue, where the Methodist church now stands. The Garden Grove Post Office was established in 1877. The building served as home to many businesses before being moved to the Stanley Ranch Museum; it is now being restored.

The Garden Grove School class of 1896 is on a picnic at the "Picnic Grove" (now Irvine Park). Merton Hill, on the lower left, became principal of the school for a few years.

Students from the first, second, and third grade of Garden Grove School pose with their teacher, Emma King, in 1898. The school had about 150 students at the time.

Garden Grove School's ninth-grade graduation class in 1903 included Ray Holley, Maude Belt, Katherine Hardy, Mary Allen, Minnie Christiansen, Della Huntington, and Carl Nichols.

Members of the 1905 student body of Garden Grove School on Euclid Street smile for the camera. The students were housed in just two rooms, so crowded classes are not a modern development.

East Side Grammar School, where Agnes Ware taught four grades, is pictured here in 1900. Agnes Ware Stanley became the benefactor of the Garden Grove Historical Society in 1970, when she deeded two acres of land to the society. The school had two rooms.

Children of East Side Grammar School, also known as Mormonville School, pose for the camera. Lilly Danforth was their teacher. Mormons settled c. 1870 in the area east and a bit south of the future Garden Grove, toward the Santa Ana River. Around 1891, they moved their church and school to what is now just east of Harbor Boulevard on Garden Grove Boulevard. The school operated under the jurisdiction of the Garden Grove Elementary School District, and stayed in use until the completion of the new Lincoln Grammar School in 1908.

In 1910, an experimental oil well was drilled on Ocean Avenue at Nelson Street. Unfortunately, oil in this area proved to be elusive.

This Garden Grove float participated in a 1912 parade in Santa Ana. The theme of the float is unknown, but the participants are well costumed.

The first graduating class from the new Lincoln Grammar School completed the ninth grade in 1909. If high school was to follow, students had to attend schools out of town until 1921.

The new Lincoln Grammar School was completed in 1908, with nine classrooms and an upstairs auditorium that could seat 250. A large school in its day, it replaced two other school buildings, the Garden Grove Grammar School on Euclid Street and the Eastside Grammar School. This photograph shows the school as it appeared in the 1920s.

The students of Mrs. Christiansen's 1911 first-grade class at Lincoln School are all dressed up for this class picture.

Chili peppers were an early crop in the Garden Grove area. In this c. 1920 photograph, Garfield and Milo Allen prepare a field for planting.

In this c. 1920 photograph, workers carry large woven baskets of chili peppers from the fields to the sorting and processing location.

A field crew takes a few minutes to pose for this c. 1920 photograph. Field boxes are filled and then taken to the stringing area.

In this c. 1920 photograph, ladies prepare and string chili peppers to be placed in drying sheds or hung on outside racks for drying. When Garden Grove Union High School started in 1921, the athletic teams were known as the Chili Peppers.

A wagon load of chili peppers is hauled to the drying shed located behind the team. Gas heaters were used in the process, and shed fires were all too common. This usually meant that the shed had to be rebuilt completely. This photograph is from the 1920s.

Harry Jentges owned the Garden Grove Cement and Pipe Company. His workmen, Jay Fry and Ed Schneider, are pictured around 1910 making cement irrigation pipes for use in bringing water from wells to the fields.

Members of the Epworth League from the Garden Grove Methodist Episcopal Church enjoy an outing at Tent City in Huntington Beach in 1916. The camp was located between Orange and Acacia Avenues and Eleventh and Thirteenth Streets. The Southern California Methodist Association operated the Tent City campsite during the summers of 1905–1920. As many as 15,000 people gathered to participate in Bible studies and to hear major speakers.

First County Y. M. C. A. Building West of Rockies, Garden Grove, Cal.

Garden Grove boasted the first county YMCA building west of the Rocky Mountains. It was established prior to World War I and was used extensively as a meeting hall for the community. Garden Grove's first library, founded by the Woman's Civic Club, occupied part of the building until 1924, when it moved across the street to share a building with the chamber of commerce. A McDonald's now occupies this lot at Walnut Street and Garden Grove Boulevard.

A large crowd gathers at the intersection of Euclid Street and Ocean Avenue to celebrate the upcoming paving of Euclid Street in 1912.

This 1912 photograph looks east on Ocean Avenue at Euclid Street and shows the "wigwag" railway crossing warning and the barrel street divider. (Courtesy of Juanita Off.)

This 1933 photograph of Euclid Street looks south from Ocean Avenue, showing freshly painted parking space stripes on the left and the Seventh-day Adventist Church on the right. (Courtesy of Don Dobmeier.)

The Pacific Electric Railway came to Garden Grove in 1905, and the depot, pictured here c. 1917, was built shortly thereafter. The completion of the railway was an economic boon for the community. Passenger service lasted until July 2, 1950. The station continued in use for several years as a pickup point for less-than-carload freight. Even that eventually faded, and the station became the hub for the local taxi company. The station was finally abandoned by 1966 and was offered to any group that wanted it, but the building had to be moved. The Garden Grove Historical Society was forming at the time and tried to save the structure, but funding and a location could not be obtained. The building was torn down by the end of 1966. The Southern Pacific Railroad continued freight service until 1977. The right-of-way still exists and is owned by the Orange County Transit Authority.

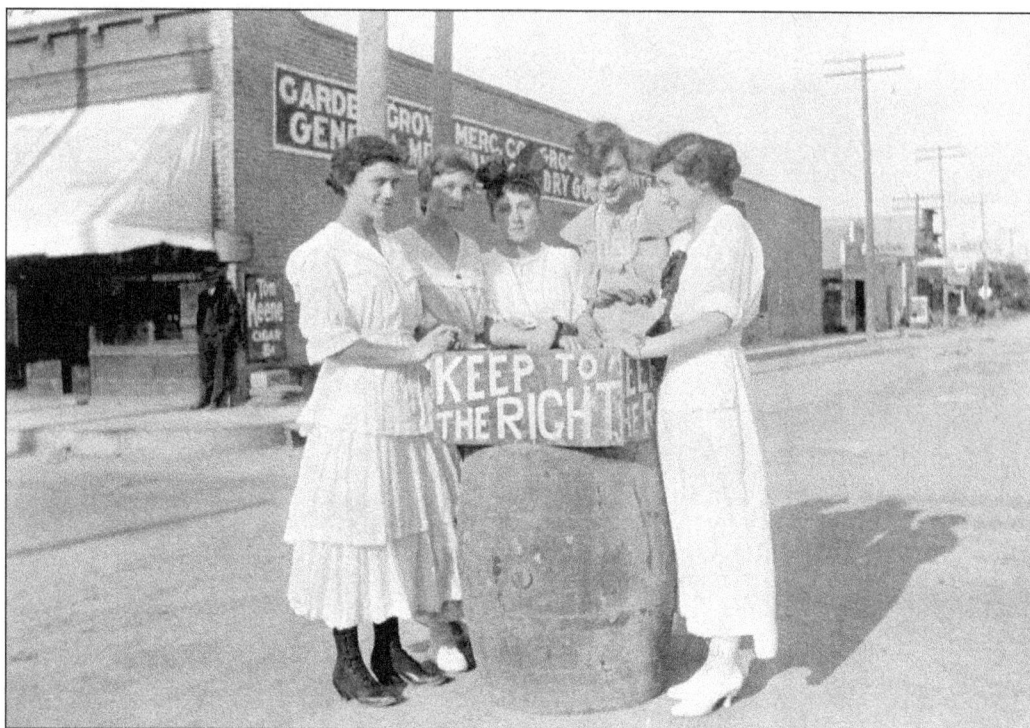

Winifred Adland, Muriel Arkley, Georgena German, Olive Northcross, and Constance German show off a unique barrel street divider at Euclid Street and Ocean Avenue, *c.* 1916.

In this *c.* 1920 photograph, the Dungan family lays walnuts out in trays for drying in the sun. The walnuts had to be turned daily. (Courtesy of Juanita Off.)

After walnuts were dried and the husks removed, they were put into burlap sacks and taken to the Walnut Packing House located next to the railroad. This wagonload of walnuts is on its way from the Schnitger Ranch in 1913.

By 1920, the Schnitger family owned this Reo truck in which they could transport walnuts—a great improvement over the horse-drawn wagon shown above.

The Preston Family Store was one of the early family-owned grocery stores. This c. 1909 view of the store's interior shows George Reyburn, Elmer Preston, a stock boy, and Delbert Preston.

Alan Knapp, shown around 1920 in his early touring car with the carbide generator on the running board, was known as the "Chili King." He was the owner and operator of many chili drying sheds and had a chili warehouse next to the railroad depot.

As farming developed in Garden Grove, more irrigation water was necessary. The first pumping plant, started in 1907 by the Allen family, was located on Euclid Street about one block south of Chapman Avenue and supplied several ranches.

A glimpse of Garden Grove Cal.

This view of the east side of Euclid Street (dating sometime prior to 1912 because of the dirt road) shows some early stores.

Fred Andre, Will Schnitger, Arthur Schnitger, Sam Gibson, and Ed Dozier pose, in 1918, with a tractor also used for power in threshing beans.

Men work with a threshing machine beside a stack of bean straw. Lima beans were separated out and placed in 100-pound sacks for transport to the Garden Grove Bean Warehouse.

The Garden Grove Bean Warehouse was located west of Main Street, off Garden Grove Boulevard, on a railroad spur. The warehouse stood for many years after beans no longer were processed, and was used by several businesses. This photograph shows the building in 1972.

Inside the Garden Grove Bean Warehouse around 1920, workers cull beans.

The Garden Grove Improvement Association entered this car float in a 1912 parade. Dr. C.C. Violette is at the wheel of his 1909 Reo. At his left is W.M. Jencks. In the rear seat, from left to right, are George Woodruff, F.J. Cloyes, and ? McElree.

The 1912 Garden Grove Improvement Association parade (to celebrate the upcaoming paving) reaches the corner of Euclid Street and Ocean Avenue.

In this c. 1915 photograph, members of the Garden Grove Improvement Association are all dressed up for one of their many activities. They include, from left to right, (front row) W. Dungan Jr.; (back row) Mr. C. Natland, Mr. Nelson, Mr. Elmore, Mr. Lake, Mr. W. Dungan, and Mr. Peler.

The Garden Grove baseball team poses in 1913 with Mr. Emerson, team manager and owner of the hardware store.

In January 1916, heavy rain caused severe flooding in Garden Grove. The flood waters are knee high in this Euclid Street photograph.

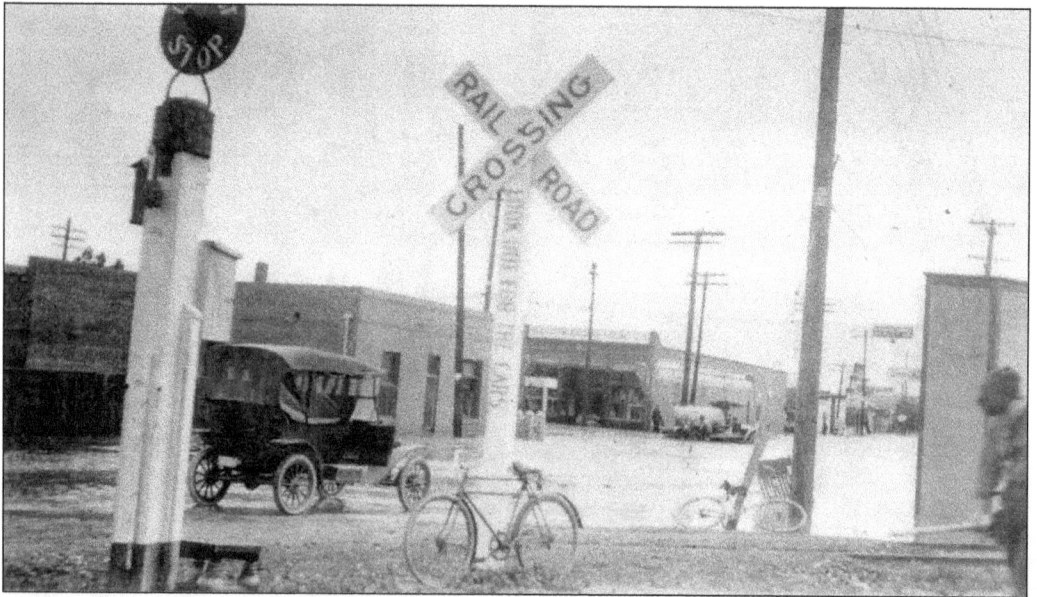

The corner of Euclid Street and Ocean Avenue was severely flooded in 1916 because of the raised railroad embankment that bisected the town.

The 1916 flood waters backed up behind the railroad embankment, which went through the center of town. No drainage had been provided when the track was laid in 1905 on the 3½-foot embankment.

Another view of the 1916 flood waters shows the problems facing local merchants and the damage to their businesses.

To eliminate the pressure caused by the flood, a decision was made (without the railroad's consent) to blow holes in the railroad embankment in four places to allow a drainage path for the water. Meeting with the railroad afterwards, the town officials received permission to lower the roadbed through town. Even today, evidence of this can be seen on the right-of-way. (Courtesy of Thelma Shields.)

48

In this photograph taken around 1910, the Lott family crosses Santiago Creek on an outing to Orange County Park. Gilbert and Ruth are in the front seat, while Frances, Esther, and Clara sit in the rear.

Miss Chaffee, the teacher, poses with her 1914–1915 class at Lincoln School.

Young women of Garden Grove work on a 1917 Red Cross drive.

Walter Dungan, Travis Anderson, and Fay Barnett pose in 1917 wearing World War I togs.

The Garden Grove Lumber and Cement Company, started in 1905 by W.M. Jencks, was purchased in 1910 by H.A. Lake (pictured on the left) and continued in business into the 1980s at the same location. The front office is now located at the Stanley Ranch Museum.

The Garden Grove Lumber and Cement Company's yard was a busy place in the 1920s. Most of the lumber was brought into the yard by rail on a spur track. The business was located on Garden Grove Boulevard, just west of Euclid Street at Taft Street. The area is now part of the Costco parking lot.

This view, looking north at Ocean Avenue, shows Euclid *c.* 1911, prior to street paving. The First National Bank is on the left, and Junkin & Keeler is on the right.

The Garden Grove Hotel, pictured here in 1912, was located near the southeast corner of Euclid Street and Ocean Avenue but the two-story building burned down in 1928.

Two

THE VILLAGE
BECOMES A TOWN
1920–1946

This interior view of the Junkin and Keeler Hardware Store, which opened in 1907 as the Mercantile Company, was captured c. 1916.

Garden Grove Grammar School's students appear here with their teacher, Harriet Brown, in 1922. Note the cultural diversity of the students.

The Garden Grove High School band is pictured here in its second year, 1922–1923. The corner of one of three original bungalows built in 1921 for the high school shows on the left.

54

The Woman's Civic Club was organized in November 1921 with 84 members and Mrs. W.T. Kirvin serving as the first president. In this 1924 photograph, members pose before their newly completed clubhouse, which was located on Garden Grove Boulevard, just west of Nelson Street, and cost $6,600.

The current home of the Woman's Civic Club is located at the corner of Gilbert Street and Chapman Avenue and was built in 1955. This photograph was taken in 2005.

This *c*. 1922 interior view of the Electric Shoe Shop of Garden Grove shows J.E. Crawford, proprietor, with his shoe machinery. The store later became a barbershop.

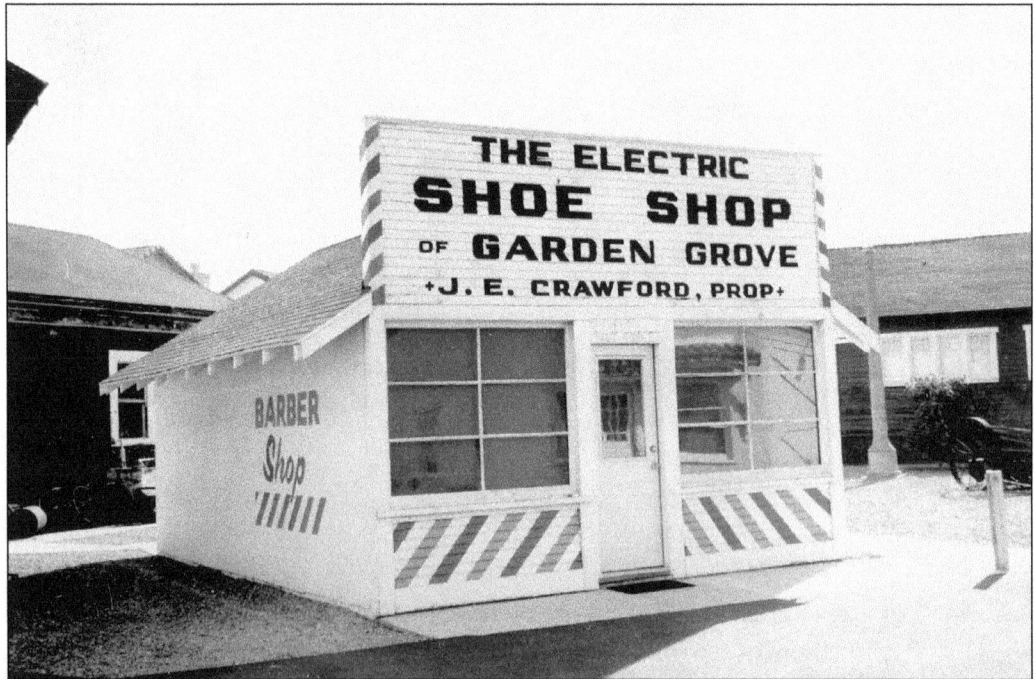

Crawford's shop was relocated to the Stanley Ranch Museum in 1974 and has been restored to display early shoe repair and barber and dental equipment. This is how it looked in 2003.

Pictured in 1918 in front of the First National Bank, located at Euclid Street and Ocean Avenue, are J.M. Woodworth, Mr. ? Cloyes, and Ed Schneider. A horse watering fountain appears on the left.

John Deickman and Frank Monroe are pictured in 1920 inside the First National Bank. Note the spittoons on the floor.

In this 1920s photograph, an orange-picking crew works in a Garden Grove orchard with their picking sacks, field boxes, and tall ladders.

Emerson Stanley, J. Lewis Dalton, and Dorothy Dalton are pictured in 1925 on the Stanley Ranch orchard (40 acres on the southeast corner of Euclid Street and Chapman Avenue).

58

Smudge pots were used to heat orange orchards during the winter months when temperatures dropped below freezing. The smoke and soot from the burning oil was not liked by residents locally or in surrounding communities. This photograph dates from the 1930s.

A load of oranges is on its way from the Dungan Ranch to the packing house c. 1917. (Courtesy of Juanita Off.)

In this *c.* 1930 photo, oranges are packed for shipment in the Garden Grove Mutual Orange Distributors Packing House, also known as the Mutual Orange Distributors (MOD).

This label for the Sunflower brand of Washington navel oranges is on the crates being packed in the photograph above.

The Garden Grove Pride (Valencias) were packed by the Garden Grove Orange Cooperative Mutual Packing House (or MOD).

Workers from the Garden Grove Mutual Packing Company gather outside the packing house during the 1920s.

This is a 1923 view of Ocean Avenue looking east near Euclid Street. The First National Bank is on the left, with the Schneider store behind it. (Courtesy of Juanita Off.)

In 1921, E.R. Schneider purchased the Junkin and Keeler Store. The shop's name was changed and the two adjoining stores provided a full range of needed goods, from hardware and paint to groceries and more.

Hubert Head (on the left) and Ed Schneider appear inside the Schneider store in 1935. The Schneider family operated the store until 1950.

From left to right, Lloyd Crane, Clara Bass, and Thomas Devine are pictured inside the Garden Grove Bakery in 1924.

The Fairchild family operated a dairy on Trask Avenue for many years. Their slogan was "No Better Food Than Milk." Fairchild and his children stand in front of one of the delivery trucks in this c. 1925 photograph.

The Sunkist Garden Grove Citrus Association building and workers came out for this picture in 1929. The refrigerator cars on the left will be loaded with oranges.

Pictured here is the Cinderella crate label for the Citrus Association (Sunkist).

Chief Gene Tobias shows off Garden Grove's first volunteer fire department and the new 1926 La France engine.

Members of the 1941 First Aid Squad stand before the Garden Grove Fire Department building on Garden Grove Boulevard near Pearl Street.

The Sun Garden Fire Department was located on Dale Street near Garden Grove Boulevard, and was operated by volunteers from 1946 until the 1956 incorporation of Garden Grove. The building still stands.

A car decorated with flags and garlands for a parade by the Woman's Civic Club in 1923 is displayed in front of Aabel's Garage on Ocean Avenue.

Garden Grove's new high school is pictured here *c.* 1925. During the March 10 earthquake, the entrance collapsed. A 13-year-old student named Elizabeth Pollard was struck and killed by the falling debris. Fortunately, the quake occurred around 6 p.m. and most students had already left school.

Garden Grove High School music instructor Alice Thornberg presents her 1924 boys' band.

In 1930, a new auditorium/gymnasium was added to Garden Grove High School (pictured here in 1948).

Pictured in 1925 are members of GGHS's Class A football team, the Chili Peppers.

Lincoln Grammar School, shown here in 1940, was torn down in the late 1940s to make way for a new and larger facility.

George Washington School, completed in 1924, was renamed the Stephen R. Fitz School in 1938 when Fitz retired as principal. The school on Acacia Avenue and Seventh Street was vacated and closed in 1948 due to safety reasons. The building was constructed prior to the March 10, 1933 Long Beach Earthquake, though it suffered little or no damage during that event.

Downtown Garden Grove was a busy place, as this c. 1925 photograph, looking north on Euclid Street, clearly shows.

A similar view of downtown Garden Grove in the 1940s shows the area after it was rebuilt following the 1933 earthquake. Along this part of downtown, a Spanish style of architecture was followed in the rebuilding.

Garden Grove's water tower, constructed in 1926, was located behind the fire station on Garden Grove Boulevard on the site that is now the Home Depot parking lot. The tower was dismantled on July 29, 1969, as part of the City's redevelopment plan. This photograph was taken just prior to the demolition.

This was Garden Grove's entry in the 1925 Orange County Fair. Pacific Electric presented it with the Sweepstakes trophy for Community Exhibits.

Walter Elliott drills a water well near Acacia Avenue and Fourth Street in this photograph from around 1900.

Alamitos School students sit for their picture in 1920.

This Euclid Street scene, looking north from Garden Grove Boulevard, shows the First National Bank prior to 1933.

E.S. Littlejohn's car, sitting near the First National Bank, was damaged during the earthquake. The quake occurred at about 6 p.m. on March 10, 1933, and is known as the Long Beach Earthquake. Long Beach is approximately 15 miles west of Garden Grove.

The March 10, 1933 earthquake changed this corner and affected many other businesses on Euclid Street and Garden Grove Boulevard. The facade and roof structure of the bank collapsed.

The First National Bank was reconstructed in a new style following the earthquake. The rebuilding of the downtown area generally followed a Spanish style of architecture.

Much work was required to bring central Garden Grove back to normal. This view is of the south side of Garden Grove Boulevard, looking east from Euclid Street. The two-story structure on the right is the Price Building. Note the post office in the center.

This section of downtown, along Garden Grove Boulevard, shows more earthquake damage. The initial estimated damage in 1933 was over $100,000. Cleanup started immediately, and repairs to the less-damaged buildings were well along within a week. The quake caused considerable damage to many other towns and cities in Orange and Los Angeles Counties.

Shopkeepers set up their tables along Euclid Street after the earthquake. The rubble had been cleaned, but the buildings had not been declared safe for reentry.

As a result of the quake, the Garr home separated in half. This type of damage inspired a new Southern California building code requirement—structures would now have to be bolted to a concrete foundation.

The Sunkist Packing House shows the damage caused by the 1933 earthquake. The building was repaired and used into the 1980s.

The roof collapsed on the MOD Packing House as a result of the quake. It was rebuilt so well that when it was to be redeveloped in the 1980s, the demolition contractor had an extremely difficult time demolishing it.

78

Preparations are made for delivering Christmas mail on December 23, 1934. Mabel Head, pictured in front, was the postmistress at the time.

Located on Garden Grove Boulevard and Verano Street was the Verano Service Station. Proprietor D.B. "Lucky" Baldwin (in white) is pictured with Al Simmons in 1934. Customers could choose either Rocket, Union '76, or Standard gas.

Garden Grove High School was remodeled to a single story after suffering damage in the 1933 earthquake. The building is now called Argo Hall and contains historical material related to the high school, which has expanded and surrounds this building today.

Air observation at Haster Air Field on Trask Avenue was performed throughout World War II. Women reported planes flying overhead during daytime hours and men worked the night hours. From left to right are Winifred German, Roland Rosselot, and Wesley Lamb.

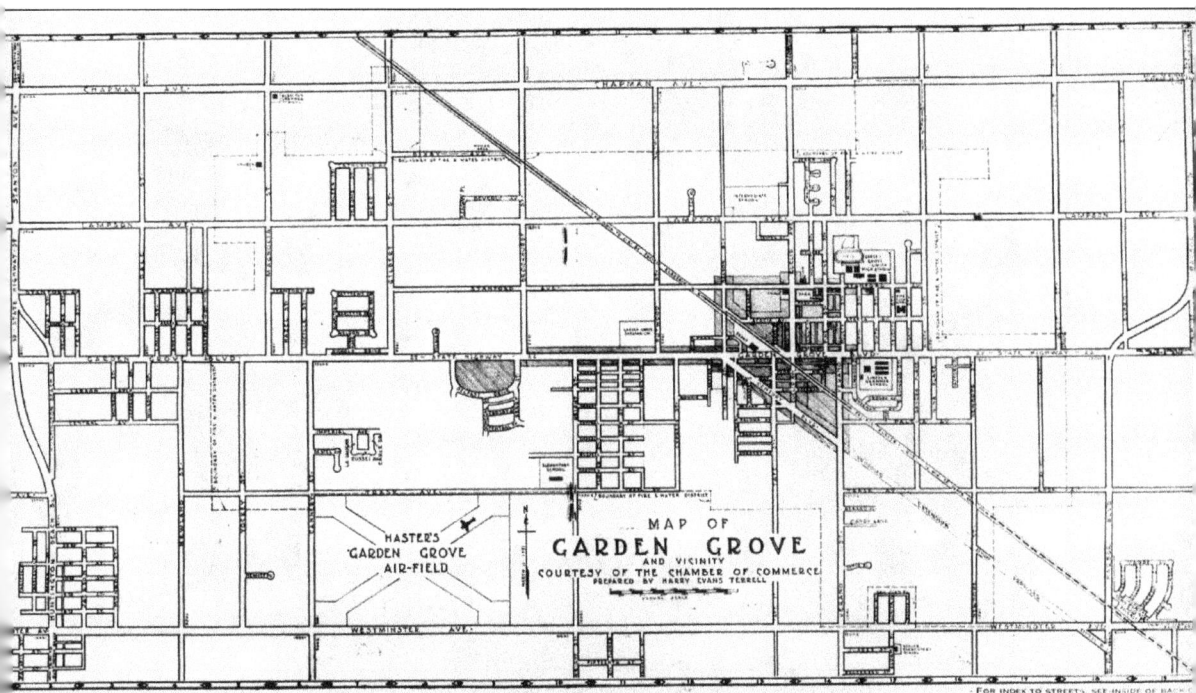

This 1949 map of the Garden Grove area shows Haster Air Field, which was rarely used and existed primarily for emergency landings. The diagonal line through the map is the Pacific Electric Railway (Southern Pacific). The shorter diagonal line just below the railway is Century Boulevard, which was to parallel the tracks as they came from Los Angeles. This never happened, as only bits and pieces were completed. The street running through the center of the map, from left to right, is Garden Grove Boulevard. Note that the streets north of Garden Grove Boulevard do not line up with the streets south of it. This was a result of township surveys in the 1860s and 1870s not matching up properly. Garden Grove Boulevard was the dividing line for these surveys, though it did not exist at that time. As seen on the left side, Beach Boulevard had a curved section constructed to join the misaligned streets as well as Harbor Boulevard (on the right side of the map). Since 1949, other major north-south streets have been joined with curved sections such as Magnolia Street, Brookhurst Street, and Euclid Street. These were done mostly in the 1960s. The streets below Garden Grove Boulevard became Magnolia Street, Wright Street became Brookhurst Street, and Verano Street became Euclid Street.

Local residents gather for the Orange County convention of the Women's Christian Temperance Union (WCTU) in 1939. The WCTU was active in Garden Grove for many years.

The Butler sisters ride a decorated horse drawn wagon in the first-annual Grover's Day parade on September 30, 1939.

The Telephone Company building was located on Euclid Street in the downtown area for many years and was still in use when this 1972 photograph was taken.

A new Telephone Company facility was built near the southeast corner of Euclid Street and Garden Grove Boulevard and, as can be seen in this 2005 photograph, was a much larger structure to satisfy growing demand.

The Poultryman's Cooperative Association (PCA) feed mill was located on Euclid Street south of Garden Grove Boulevard on land now occupied by Costco. Originally built in 1937 by Charles Simpson as the Simpson Milling Company, it was sold to become the Bell Milling Company in the mid-1940s. By 1950, it was the PCA mill.

This scene, looking east, shows Garden Grove Boulevard in the late 1960s. The two-story building at the Euclid Street intersection is the Price Building. Garden Grove Boulevard has since been widened, and none of these buildings exist today.

A facility for the new Honold's Mortuary was constructed on Garden Grove Boulevard in 1940. The business was formed by Ben and George Honold, father and son. Around 1980, they moved to Chapman Avenue, just west of Nelson Street.

A building located behind the mortuary became known as "Honold's Hut" and was available to local groups as a meeting facility until the late 1970s when the property was redeveloped.

The congregation of Garden Grove Methodist Episcopal Church first met in November 1875 at the home of A.G. Cook, Garden Grove's founder. An 1879 church building they constructed was enlarged in 1894 and is pictured here.

On February 26, 1967, a consecration service was held for the fourth sanctuary of the Methodist Church on Main Street at Stanford Avenue. It was constructed using poured concrete to create its unusual shape.

Among the earliest churches in town was the Alamitos Friends Church on Magnolia Avenue, which dedicated this new building on October 28, 1923.

On September 14, 1941, the Alamitos Friends Church members gathered to commemorate their 50th anniversary with this picture of the congregation standing in front of the church.

The Orange County Public Library moved to this location at 12651 Euclid Street in April 1952. It was here for 17 years and expanded twice during that time to a total of 3,000 square feet. Ruth Wentz was librarian until 1961 and was followed by Jennie Mae Robinson and then Lillian Neal. A telephone was installed in 1953.

On September 13, 1969, a new facility for the Orange County Public Library, the Garden Grove Regional Library, was dedicated and opened to the public. The library is located on two floors with a total of 21,000 square feet of space. Mrs. Catherine Spencer became librarian for the new facility. This was the first building to be constructed in the new community center development for Garden Grove.

A unique double groundbreaking ceremony was held in 1963 to launch two new Orange County branch libraries to meet the needs of an increasing population. Commemorating the event are, from left to right, Mrs. Jennie Robinson (Euclid Branch Library), Robert Main (president of the Garden Grove Friends of the Library), Mrs. Kay Walton (assistant county librarian), Mrs. Margaret Morrison (county librarian), county supervisor C.M. Featherly, Mayor George Honold, and county supervisor David Baker.

Opening ceremonies for the two new branch libraries took place simultaneously on January 14, 1964. Shown here is the Chapman branch, identical to the West Garden Grove branch.

The Greenbrier Inn, located on Garden Grove Boulevard at Nutwood Street, was set on a 15-acre site surrounded by lush gardens. Opened in 1940, it had a sanitarium, a hotel, and a restaurant, and soon became a local landmark.

The lobby of the Greenbrier Inn displays its elegance in this 1963 photograph. The inn was closed in the 1970s, torn down, and replaced by multiple-unit housing.

Three

GROWTH AND MATURITY
1946–PRESENT

In 1956, when Garden Grove incorporated, the construction of a city hall became necessary. The Fitz School on Acacia Avenue had been vacant for about eight years and was thought to be suitable. On August 8, 1956, the City passed a resolution to acquire the school and paid $1 to the school district for the building. Over the years, extensive renovations were made to improve both the building's usability and safety. This building was torn down in 1995, when the new city hall was put into service.

This view of "downtown," taken from the intersection of Euclid Street and Garden Grove Boulevard at 8 a.m. on January 11, 1949, depicts the first snowfall in Garden Grove since 1881. The population of the city in 1949 was about 3,600 people. Bob Spurrier's 1941 Dodge appears in the foreground.

In January 1952, Garden Grove was flooded by heavy rains. Unloading mail from the truck are Neil Sprinkle and Joe Ryan (with hat).

On Friday, January 18, 1952, the Garden Grove Post Office at 11068 Garden Grove Boulevard was flooded, but postal employees carried on sorting mail while the water level continued to rise. Neil Sprinkle is on the left. Note the knee boots and bare feet.

This *c.* 1960 photograph shows the recreation building in Euclid Park, now known as the Village Green, between Euclid and Main Streets. (Courtesy of Don Dobmeier.)

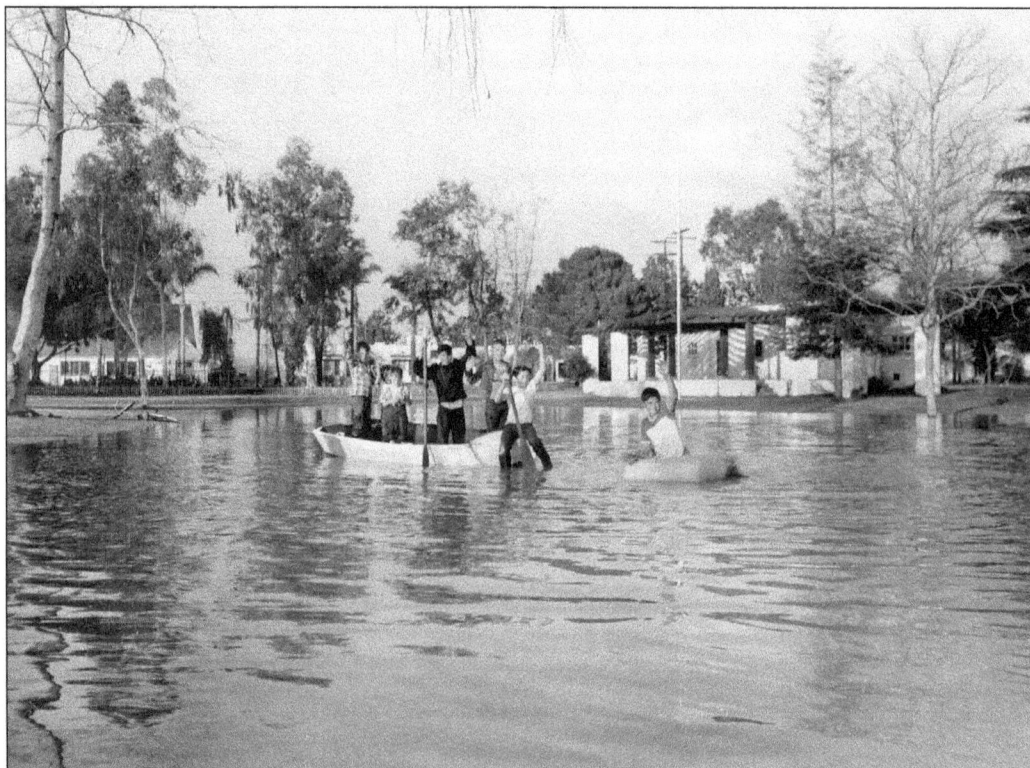

In February 1969, flooding occurred again, covering Euclid Park with water, and residents turned the problem into an opportunity for a boat ride through the park.

94

A resident enjoys waterskiing on a Garden Grove street during the 1969 flood.

The 1950s brought a housing boom to Garden Grove. A new tract of homes is under construction in this photograph.

The Garden Grove city limit sign in 1952 indicated a population of 3,762.

The housing boom brought many changes to the city. Mail carrier Harold Davis is pictured on his postal bike at Brookhurst and Westminster Boulevard by Garden Grove's city limit sign, which shows a population increase to 84,417 in 1961.

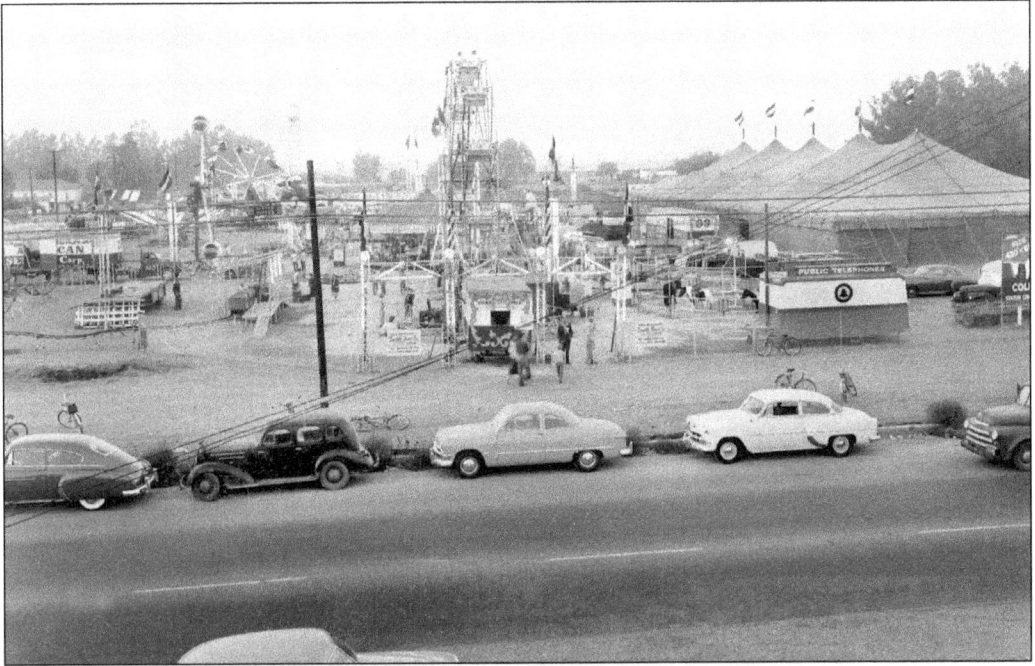

The first-annual Grover's Day was held on September 30, 1939. By 1953, a full-scale festival had evolved. Later, the event became the Strawberry Festival. This photograph shows the festivities at Garden Grove Boulevard and Nutwood Street.

The Garden Grove High School band participated in the 1955 Grover's Day parade on Euclid Street.

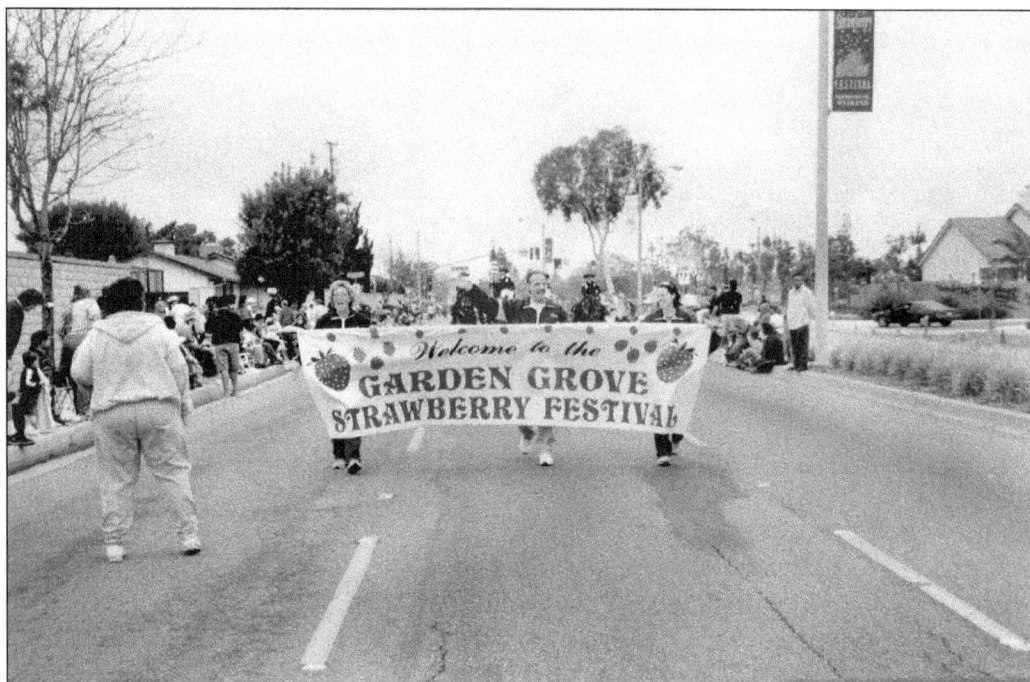

Pictured in 2002 is the banner for the Strawberry Festival parade, held every year on Saturday of Memorial Day weekend.

In this 2002 photograph, a patriotic float travels along Euclid Street on the Strawberry Festival parade route.

Pictured at the 2002 Strawberry Festival parade, Ronald McDonald rides in a mid-1920s Model T Ford past the Ware-Stanley House at the Stanley Ranch Museum.

A 2002 aerial photograph (taken from the Ferris wheel) shows a corner of the Strawberry Festival grounds. The new city clock tower is in the distance.

This 1950s aerial view of downtown, at Garden Grove Boulevard and Euclid Street, shows the Pacific Electric tracks cutting diagonally through town, as well as many businesses and packing houses. The Sunkist Packing House is on the right side. The station is the Garden Grove Boulevard–adjacent building on the left of the tracks. The MOD packing house is just above the station, and the building above the MOD in the upper-left corner is the volunteer fire department station.

This map, made sometime between 1905 and 1915, shows tract boundaries, as well as industrial and commercial areas.

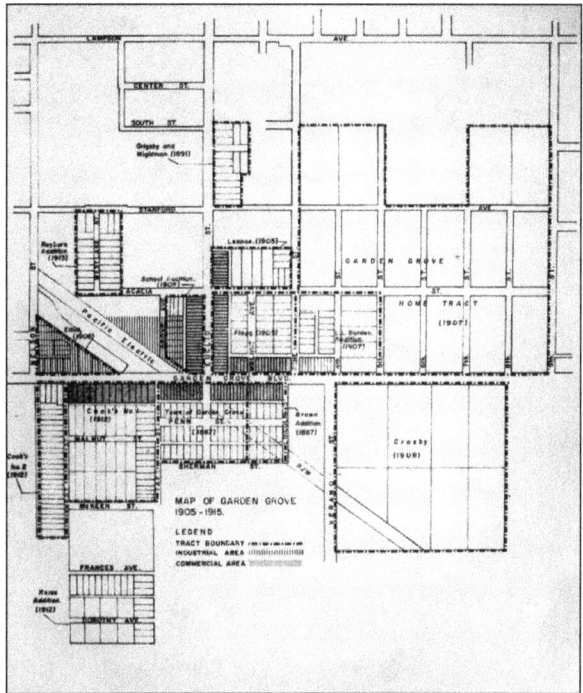

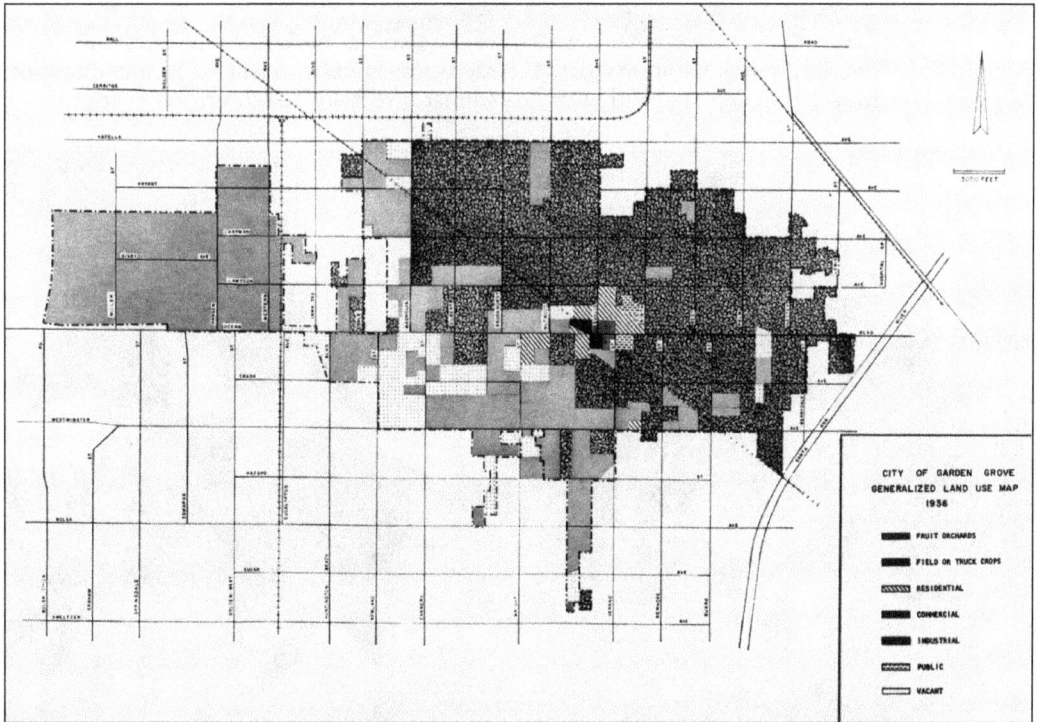

Garden Grove's generalized land use map of 1936 details fruit orchards, field and truck crops, and residential, commercial, industrial, public, and vacant areas. The map also predicts the future, showing areas to the west that were not annexed until many years later after the city was incorporated in 1956.

A June 20, 1956 aerial photograph shows part of Garden Grove just two days after its incorporation as a city. The intersection depicted is that of Brookhurst Street and Westminster Avenue.

A polo match is underway in Garden Grove, c. 1960, at the polo field on Garden Grove Boulevard between Casa Linde Lane and Cannery Street. Polo was played for many years at this location. (Photograph by Al Carr; courtesy of Gerlinde Carr.)

On January 31, 1958, members of the Auld Lang Syne Club—all of whom attended the Garden Grove School on Euclid Street—met on the front steps of the Chaffee home. The club still exists today, and members meet quarterly for luncheons and programs. Those in the front row later taught at Garden Grove School. Pictured, from left to right, are (front row) Merton Hill, Mary Moody, Carrie Small, Agnes Stanley, and Clara Boyer; (middle row) Lenore Wilson, Burns Chaffee, Mabel Lowell, and Herman Christensen; (back row) Mettie Chaffee, Estelle Harper, Helen Schitger, Roy Olfield, Rose Hill, Leila Srigley, Carrie Hill, and Arthur Schnitger.

Pictured center, councilwoman Kay Barr and mayor George Honold participate in the Air Force dedication of a cargo plane named the *City of Garden Grove*.

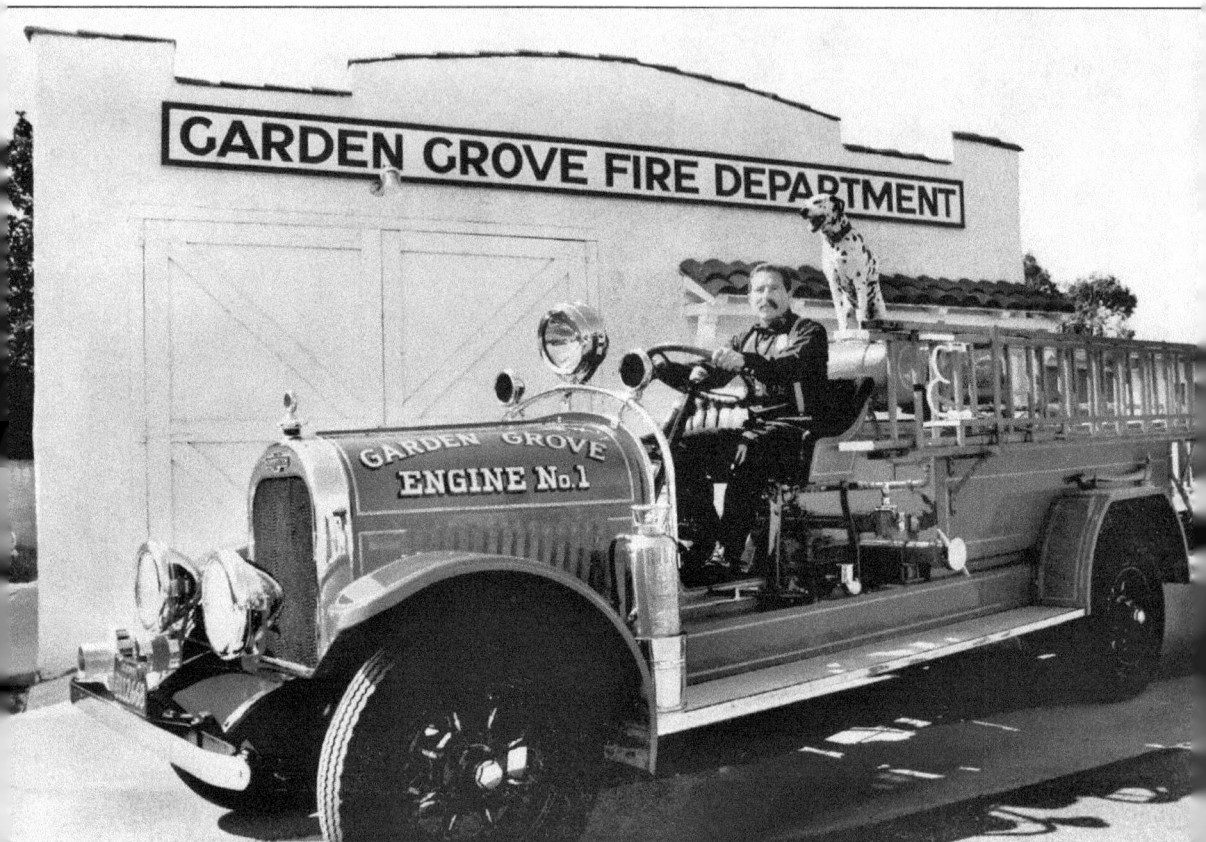

This 2000 photograph shows Garden Grove's very first 1926 La France after restoration. Fireman Dean Taylor and mascot Sparky display the engine in front of the Garden Grove Historical Society's replica of the original fire station at Stanley Ranch Museum. The engine is used in parades and at city functions and may be viewed during tours at Stanley Ranch Museum. The engine was restored over a period of several years in the 1980s, with most of the work done at the museum. Leonard Zerlaut headed up the restoration project with assistance from Neil Sprinkle and Kenneth Hall. Through the efforts of historical society member Fred Coles, the engine was brought to the museum in 1974 from a storage site at one of Garden Grove's fire stations. Coles worked with the fire department to assure its home at the Stanley Ranch Museum. The fire department and Fireman's Association have contributed material and equipment to the engine to help return it to its original equipped condition.

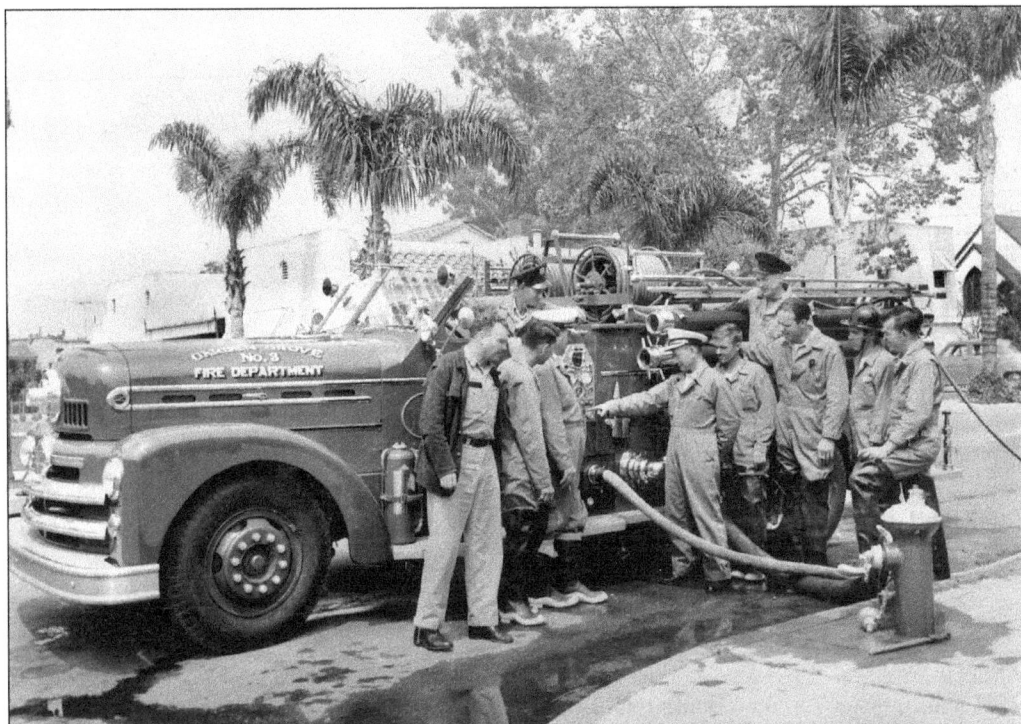

The Garden Grove Volunteer Fire Department shows off their Engine No. 3 in 1953.

The crew for Garden Grove Fire Station No. 2 posed for this photograph in March 1959.

Atlantis Park, a three-acre children's fantasy play center, opened on June 29, 1963, at 9301 Westminster Avenue. Built around the legend of a city beneath the sea, the park boasted unique play equipment, including this pirate ship and a sea serpent. The concept, planning, and coordination of the project were handled by the Junior Woman's Civic Club of Garden Grove.

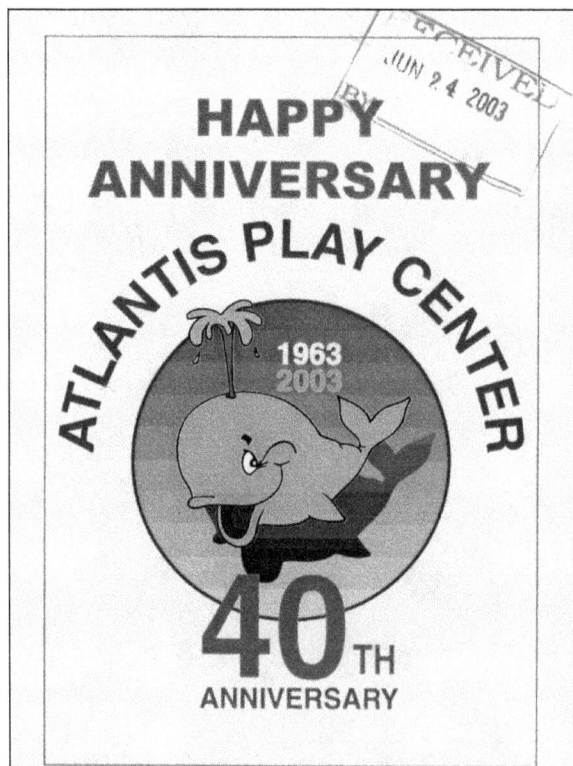

A celebration of the 40th anniversary of the Atlantis Play Center (as it is now known) was held on June 29, 2003.

The opening of the Garden Grove Freeway took place on December 23, 1965, and dedication ceremonies included a parade of old cars, speeches, a band, and even a visit from Santa Claus. (Courtesy of the State of California, Department of Public Works, Division of Highway District 7.)

In this c. 1960 photograph, the congregation of the Foursquare Church gathers in front of their building on Century Boulevard.

From about 1925, the Garden Grove Post Office occupied space in the Price Building on the southeast corner of Garden Grove Boulevard and Euclid Street. After three moves to adjacent store space along Garden Grove Boulevard in the Price Building block, this location at 11068 Garden Grove Boulevard was occupied in 1951, when this photograph was taken. The post office moved in 1956 to 10632 Garden Grove Boulevard, near Century Boulevard and Nutwood Street.

In 1967, a dedication ceremony was held for the new Garden Grove Post Office at Nutwood Street and Stanford Avenue. This much larger facility has served the city since that time.

Members of Garden Grove's baseball team, still known as the Chili Peppers, show off their uniforms in 1948.

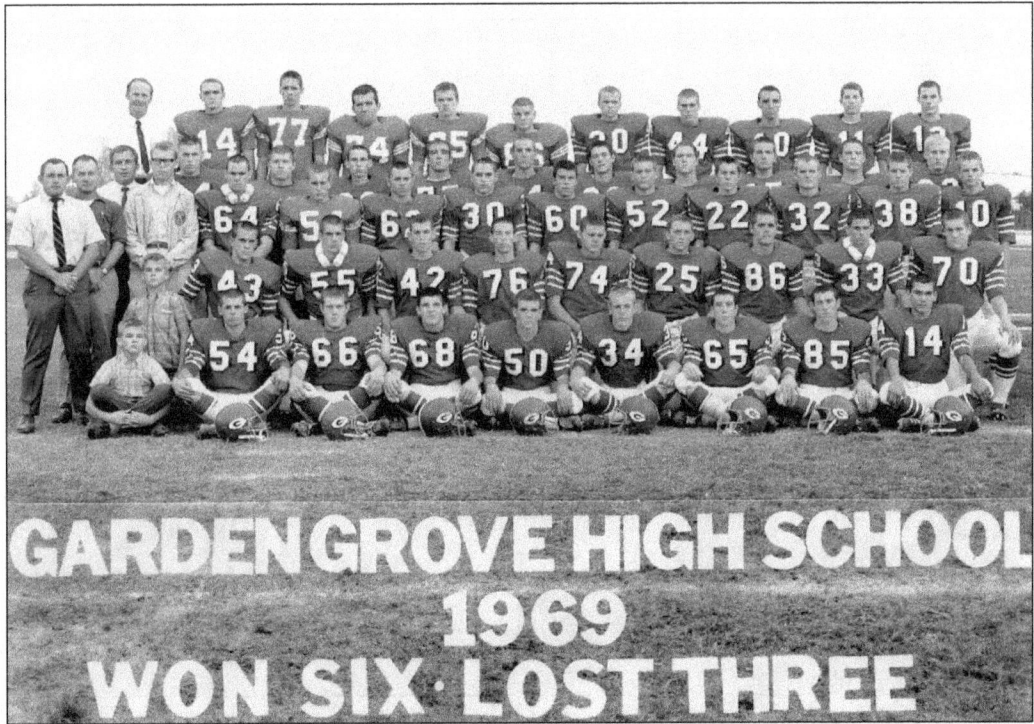

Team members and coaches of the Garden Grove High School football team are pictured in 1969. By this time, the teams were the Argonauts (or Argos, for short).

This original building of the First Baptist Church was situated at the corner of Stanford Avenue and Pine Street. Formed on February 13, 1897, with 24 charter members, the church was first located where the Pacific Electric Depot was later built, and moved to a location on the south side of Garden Grove Boulevard near Lincoln Street when the railroad came through town. In 1914, the congregation found a permanent home at the Stanford Avenue location.

Pictured in 2000 is the First Baptist Church at Euclid Street and Stanford Avenue. This is the same location as the photograph at the top of this page, but the 1960s relocation of Euclid Street caused the street name change.

The parish of St. Columban Catholic Church constructed this building at Fourth Street and Stanford Avenue in 1946. Membership growth brought with it the need for larger facilities and so property was purchased on Stanford Avenue at Nelson Street. A church was built in 1953, and the Fourth Street building became the parish's social hall. Garden Grove bought this property in 1965 to realign Euclid Street.

This 2005 photograph shows the newest St. Columban sanctuary, which was built in 1967. The first mass was celebrated here on April 21, 1968. The earlier building had been named in honor of Msgr. Michael J. Murphy, the founding pastor, and became the social hall. The church is located at the northeast corner of Nelson Street and Stanford Avenue.

Garden Grove's famous Crystal Cathedral, located at Chapman Avenue and Lewis Street, is pictured here in 2005. The church was founded by Rev. Robert Schuller on March 27, 1955, in a drive-in movie theater. A chapel was built in 1957, and Philip Johnson designed the 2,890-seat Crystal Cathedral that was completed and dedicated on September 14, 1980.

The Chimes Tower stands near the main sanctuary building of the Crystal Cathedral.

Pictured here in 1972, a Japanese language school was built in Garden Grove the 1920s and remained in use until the late 1970s. Its former location on Penn Street near Euclid Street is now the middle of the Costco parking lot.

In 1972, students attended Saturday classes at the Japanese language school to learn the Japanese language and the country's cultural heritage.

Comdr. Donald A. Gary received the Congressional Medal of Honor from Pres. Harry S. Truman on January 23, 1946. Commander Gary received this honor for his successful rescue of men trapped below decks of the USS *Franklin* after it was struck by the Japanese during World War II. Commander Gary was a longtime resident of Garden Grove.

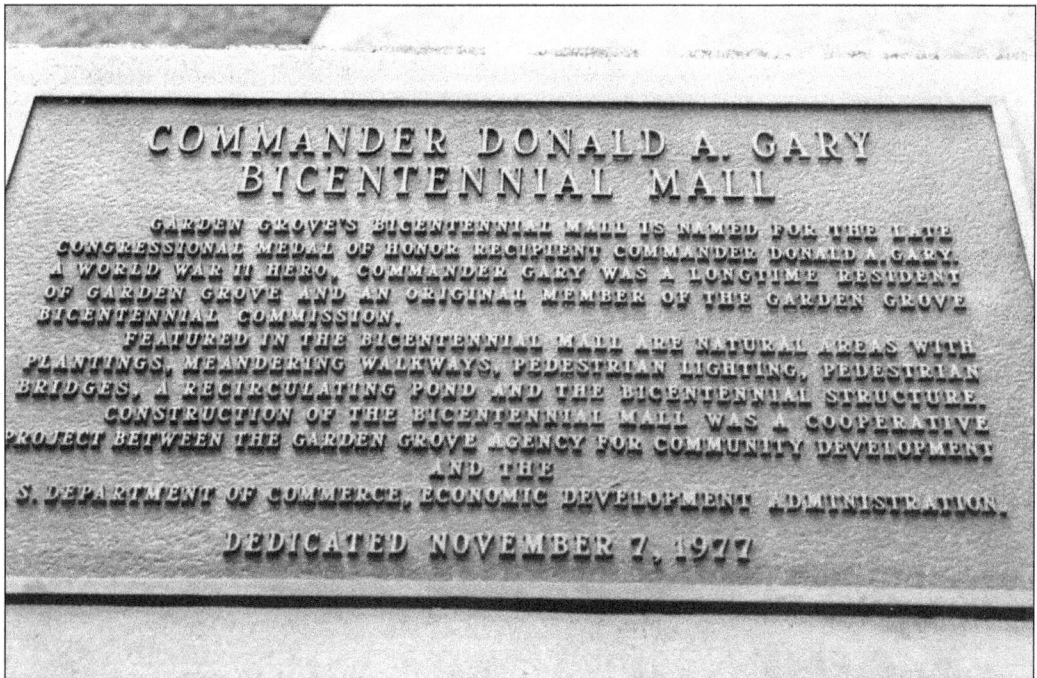

COMMANDER DONALD A. GARY
BICENTENNIAL MALL

GARDEN GROVE'S BICENTENNIAL MALL IS NAMED FOR THE LATE
CONGRESSIONAL MEDAL OF HONOR RECIPIENT COMMANDER DONALD A. GARY,
A WORLD WAR II HERO. COMMANDER GARY WAS A LONGTIME RESIDENT
OF GARDEN GROVE AND AN ORIGINAL MEMBER OF THE GARDEN GROVE
BICENTENNIAL COMMISSION.
    FEATURED IN THE BICENTENNIAL MALL ARE NATURAL AREAS WITH
PLANTINGS, MEANDERING WALKWAYS, PEDESTRIAN LIGHTING, PEDESTRIAN
BRIDGES, A RECIRCULATING POND AND THE BICENTENNIAL STRUCTURE.
    CONSTRUCTION OF THE BICENTENNIAL MALL WAS A COOPERATIVE
PROJECT BETWEEN THE GARDEN GROVE AGENCY FOR COMMUNITY DEVELOPMENT
                            AND THE
S. DEPARTMENT OF COMMERCE, ECONOMIC DEVELOPMENT ADMINISTRATION.

DEDICATED NOVEMBER 7, 1977

The Comdr. Donald A. Gary Bicentennial Mall in the civic center was dedicated on November 7, 1977.

"The Eagle Has Landed" monument to Commander Gary is in a park area adjacent to the Garden Grove Regional Library on Stanford Avenue.

115

The Gem Theater, pictured here in 1972, was a local movie house known originally as the Grand Theater, then the Garden Theater, before it was renamed the Gem Theater. Construction of the building began on May 18, 1923.

Photographed in 2005 after a complete renovation during the 1980s, the Gem Theater presents plays, musicals, and other cultural events.

The home of George Mills on Euclid Street served as the Mills House Art Gallery from 1974 to 1984. This photograph shows the home as it appeared in the 1940s.

The City replaced the Mills House with a new building known as the Courtyard Center, which was used as a facility for meetings and classes.

Garden Grove's finest are pictured in their new uniforms. The department became official on June 25, 1957, and began duty on July 1, 1957. At the time of this photograph, four of the women were still waiting for some of their uniform apparel. (Courtesy of Bill Dalton.)

Garden Grove police chief Reece Ballard conducts a review of the force with a lieutenant commander from Los Alamitos Naval Air Station in front of city hall in 1958.

The Garden Grove Police Department was the first in Orange County to have a canine unit on duty. Officer Jack Trott is pictured here with his trusted companion on April 12, 1967. (Courtesy of Bill Dalton.)

The Vietnamese American Buddhist Temple on Magnolia Street, just north of Lampson Avenue, is a recent addition to Garden Grove. The temple was built in 1995 and is pictured here in 2005.

A monument and sign on Garden Grove Boulevard designate the start of the Korean business district. The Korean business community has become an integral part of Garden Grove.

A Vietnamese monument and sign welcome travelers going north on Brookhurst Street at Hazard Avenue to the "Little Saigon" business district.

The headquarters of the Islamic Society of Orange County is located on Thirteenth Street and is another example of the diverse cultural mix of Garden Grove. The site is home to the Orange Crescent School and the Mosque of Al-Rahman.

Zlaket's Market was opened in 1927 by Leo Zlaket Sr. and has continued operation under the management his sons. Pictured the store's interior during its 78th-anniversary celebration. The store is located on the west side of Main Street in the historic business district.

This is how the intersection of Garden Grove Boulevard and Main Street looks in 2005.

Garden Grove's Public Safety Building, located on the north side of Acacia Parkway and completed in 1976, houses the police and fire departments. This photograph was taken around 1980.

Formerly the headquarters of the Orange County Transit Authority, this building on the south side of Acacia Parkway was renovated and now serves as Garden Grove's city hall. Its dedication was held in November 1995.

The entrance sign for the Garden Grove Historical Society's two-acre Stanley Ranch Museum can be seen on Euclid Street between Lampson and Chapman Avenue. The museum boasts 17 buildings, half of which are open to the public; others are in various stages of renovation and restoration.

The tank house was relocated from another portion of the Stanley family property. Now attached to the tank house, the general store was originally an Orange County Water District office located at Nelson Street and Garden Grove Boulevard.

The Ware-Stanley house, built in 1892 by Edward and Mary Ware, was originally situated on a 40-acre ranch at the corner of Euclid Street and Chapman Avenue. This fully restored Victorian-era farmhouse is on Orange County's list of historic sites.

The dining room is one of eight rooms in the Ware-Stanley house on the visitor's tour. In 1971, the house was moved a few hundred feet south to its location on the two-acre grounds of the Stanley Ranch Museum.

The bell at the Garden Grove School disappeared after the school was torn down in 1908, but after the 1916 flood, it was discovered buried in mud behind the stores on Main Street. It was put on display at the Lincoln School on Garden Grove Boulevard until 1973, when it was relocated to the Stanley Ranch Museum.

Originally part of the home of Walt Disney's uncle in Los Angeles, this garage was where Walt Disney built an early animation machine. In 1982, the building was taken apart, carefully labeled, stored, and reconstructed on the Stanley Ranch Museum site in 1984. Considered Disney's first garage studio, it houses a variety of Disney-related material.

126

Arthur Schnitger's home was on the family ranch at the southwest corner of Euclid Street and Chapman Avenue. Relocated to the Stanley Ranch Museum in 1977, it has been fully restored and features a variety of displays.

The Blaeholder house was built c. 1885 on the south side of Chapman Avenue, between Nutwood Street and Nelson Street, where the Dimond and Shannon Mortuary is now located. Relocated to the Stanley Ranch Museum in 1977, the home will undergo an interior restoration.

This plaque, mounted on the base of the flagpole at the Stanley Ranch Museum, is dedicated to the Garden Grovers who lost their lives during World War II. The plaque was first placed on the bandstand in Euclid Park, but was remounted here in 1972 when the flagpole was installed.

The courtyard and gazebo of the Stanley Ranch Museum provide a quiet place for meditation. The Ware-Stanley house is visible beyond the courtyard.

Visit us at
arcadiapublishing.com

· ·

www.ingramcontent.com/pod-product-compliance
Lightning Source LLC
Chambersburg PA
CBHW050624110426
42813CB00007B/1713